Abyssinia Revisited

Copyright © Laurence Impey, 2019
Published by I_AM Self-Publishing, 2019.

The right of Laurence Impey to be identified as the Author of the Work has been asserted by him in accordance with the Copyright, Designs and Patents Act 1988.

All rights reserved.

ISBN 978-1-913036-77-5

This book is sold subject to the condition it shall not, by way of trade or otherwise, be circulated in any form or by any means, electronic or otherwise without the publisher's prior consent.

@iamselfpub
www.iamselfpublishing.com

Letters from Lalibela
November 2016 – February 2017

እንኳን ደህና መጣህ!
WELCOME!

Foreword

The average man – indeed, most probably, the greater part of the married male population – would doubtless be more than a little disturbed by his wife's suggestion, floated casually across the supper table one evening, that perhaps he should consider absenting himself from the family home for three months. Although a few long-suffering spouses might respond brightly to this surprise get-out-of-jail-free card, for the most part only the most naïve or fortunate of husbands could receive this proposal with equanimity; from deep down, dark-tinged thoughts and ill-formed suspicions are likely to surface.

So it is to the infinite credit of my wife, Belinda, that I unhesitatingly took at face value her idea that I might need more than a lengthier list of domestic duties to occupy me profitably on finally taking retirement in the spring of 2016; that I might welcome the stimulus of a little adventure as I turned seventy; that the secondary schools in Lalibela, known to us from our previous visit to the Northern Highlands of Ethiopia, might welcome three months of free teaching of English by a retired teacher of foreign languages.

The idea took root. We had, after all, on a previous trip developed a connection with Lalibela, sponsoring the education of three of its sons, one of whom, Yosef, was still at school there. A few months later, after pestering friends and acquiring a treasury of ideas for teaching English as a foreign language, I boarded, not without a little apprehension, my Ethiopian Airlines flight to Addis Ababa. The process thus far, however, had been anything but smooth, and along the way I lost the nascent title for this book. I had at no point contemplated writing a book. But having been encouraged to record my experiences, a title came to mind: "*Septuagenarian for a Day*". This might hint mysteriously at a life cut short, but its true significance is far from dark.

On boarding any plane, it is no surprise to have to adjust one's watch forward or back a number of hours. More unusual is to adjust the calendar by seven years, as is the case when flying to Ethiopia. Thus, in the space of twenty-four hours, I would have travelled back in time from 2016 to 2009, effortlessly shedding those last seven years and emerging from the plane once again a sprightly sixty-three-year-old. In the event the title was strangled at birth. My plan to fly out on the day after my seventieth birthday had to be shelved; a combination of Ethiopian bureaucracy, tribal insurgency and Foreign Office caution was responsible. "Septuagenarian for a Month" didn't have the same ring to it.

During the long wait for a resolution to these troubles I re-read Evelyn Waugh's account of his first excursion to Ethiopia, then known as Abyssinia, in 1930, an account which became a defining influence on my own observations of life in that country. Although the

Foreword

frustrated Waugh was waiting in Djibouti for a passage by rail to the Ethiopian capital, I, kicking my heels in England, was in fact, in terms of hours, closer than he was, but how I sympathised when I read his disheartened "I began to think we should never get to Addis Ababa."!

The bustling Addis Ababa I saw when I eventually arrived was very different from the parochial town described by Waugh. It was also a different place from the city I had seen three years earlier. Many of the ramshackle, low-rise buildings lining the main streets in the centre of town had been bulldozed. The sites of those which had not already been replaced by gleaming high-rise office blocks were being prepared for their transformation. Rickety scaffolding was much in evidence. Trams glided smoothly over viaducts. The number of vehicles seemed to have increased, rendering the air in the lower part of town scarcely breathable. It was, however, inadvisable to look up too much in wonder at the changed cityscape; open manholes and obstacles on the pavement were a constant hazard.

And yet, even with its twenty-first century coffee shops, Addis is still far from a European city - and long may it remain indelibly African in its essence, a melting pot of many peoples but nevertheless proudly unique. Mosques peacefully rub shoulders with churches; beggars sit hunched on the pavement while the prosperous middle classes stride by; verdant gardens entice the eye away from the dusty streets. These streets often bear two quite different names and the houses are unnumbered; an Ethiopian calendar is in use alongside a European one; there are two different versions of telling the time of day. It is frankly a minor miracle that anyone ever successfully meets anyone else at the right time of day in the right place.

Addis is a good halfway-house for those venturing into the interior of the country. After three days of acclimatisation to the altitude, the sunshine, the city's adventitious character and a unique culture which would define my three-month stay in Ethiopia, I was ready for the challenges of life in Lalibela, spiritual heart of the old Abyssinia – and, once there, soon unable to contain a desire to record what I found for all the kind and supportive friends and family who had celebrated my seventieth birthday with me and waved me off to an uncertain start to my eighth decade. Hence this collection of successive dispatches. They are, however, not a guide to the astonishing treasures of Lalibela, which can be found documented in all their fascination elsewhere. Rather it is a record of the diversity of my daily life, of aspects both mundane and outstanding. Its contents will refer at times to our three sponsored boys, our Ethiopian "sons", Yosef, Abiy and Ephraim, and will doubtless betray the innocent abroad, but also a warm regard for much of what I found there. More generally, I hope it will convey the wonder and value of travel, even, perhaps especially, when undertaken in one's declining years.

Acknowledgements

I am deeply grateful to Muriel Owen for her generous contribution of drawings, without which this slight booklet would be quite insignificant. I am also indebted to Evelyn Waugh, whose commentaries on the Abyssinia of the thirties amused, stimulated and inspired me; to Philip Briggs, whose authoritative and entertaining Bradt Guide to Ethiopia has been an invaluable companion; and lastly to my wife, Belinda, to whom many of the photographs can be attributed, and of course, without whom there would have been no adventure and no book.

Laurence Impey
Epsom, August 2018

ጤና ይስጥልኝ
GOD GIVE YOU HEALTH

Letters

1. My New Home — p. 21
2. Sunday — p. 35
3. My Schools — p. 47
4. Village Life — p. 61
5. My Gregorian Christmas — p. 75
6. My Orthodox Christmas — p. 89
7. Epiphany — p. 105
8. A Wedding — p. 119
9. A Walk in the Country — p. 131
10. You Are Old, Father Laurence — p. 142
11. A Second Wedding — p. 147
12. Goodbye to Lalibela — p. 161

My New Home

Abyssinia Revisited: Letters from Lalibela

I know I was warned, but I have indeed discovered to my inconvenience that the internet is only intermittently accessible here. I've had to tame my inner European man; I've had to develop patience, which, when comfortably sipping papaya juice, gazing out over the mountain ranges, watching buzzard-like birds circling high in the sky, proves not to be so hard. The hotels have been short of guests during this ongoing state of emergency. Rather than the protesters, it is, at least among the younger people here, the government that is getting the blame for the unrest and consequent decline in tourist numbers in the country. A few nonchalantly independent European and oriental tourists have evidently scorned official advice; none the less I am doubly welcome, even if it is only to use the hotels' wi-fi. Of course, everyone has been cheered by the news that the British and German governments have finally relaxed travel restrictions.

Very much has happened since I arrived. There has scarcely been a moment free to email, and when there has been, there's either been no internet connection or a power cut. Let me focus today on my house, because this is where my effort to adapt to my new situation has so far been concentrated. It's a one-storey building with a pitched roof on the southwestern fringe of the town, in a quiet location, only a couple of minutes from a comfortable, modern hotel set on a promontory with spectacular views. Built on the hillside on the lower side of the road, the house is accessible via stairs down from the front gate, which gives it a semi-basement feel. Currently the access is problematic, to say the least. Due to the transformation of the road from a dirt track to a cobbled road, many workmen have been engaged in digging a deep and wide trench immediately in front of the houses on this side of the road. (Economists worried about productivity would be horrified - there are no machines.) The dirt road itself is narrowed by the resultant piles of soil and rocks which this operation involves. The workmen busy themselves in a lively way with a lot of banter. Whenever they themselves have been in the trench, they have courteously offered to help me down the temporary staircase of boulders in front of the gate. Yesterday, however, I returned from school to find the "staircase" had been demolished, leaving only the sheer face of soil and rock. The workmen seemed amused, whether at my plight or at my attempts at Amharic I couldn't tell. But it seems the foreman had been sent for. He arrived with an underling armed with a hammer, and invited me to scramble up after them into the neighbour's front "garden", where they proceeded to remove a panel of the corrugated iron fence dividing the two properties. No consultation appeared to be thought necessary for this incursion and alteration. Bending double beneath the horizontal wooden rail, I regained access to my house. This novel entrance will, it seems, remain in force for the next few days.

Abyssinia Revisited: Letters from Lalibela

Entrance to my sanctuary is heralded by, on one side, an inviting-looking terrace, set with two chairs and a table, whose attraction is currently rendered less compelling by a continually evolving layer of dust from the roadworks; and on the other side, supported on sturdy wooden legs, an enlarged rabbit hutch of corrugated iron. In this latter curiosity sleeps my nocturnal guard, whose disembodied voice I heard one night. Upon opening the slightly battered metal and glass front door, one is struck by the contrast between the austerity of whitish walls and the ill-fitting, dark red carpet, of dubious antiquity, and dark furniture. Two pictures, one dark and one painted in vivid hues, of St George's church are propped up, one on the large television screen in one corner, the other atop a rickety cabinet, which has already lost one door and will doubtless fall further to pieces during my stay. It may be wise to remove the breakable china and glassware first. The furnishing of this (by Ethiopian standards) spacious sitting room is completed by two large sofas and two large armchairs, hideous but surprisingly comfortable; a glass-topped coffee table, which, when we needed to move it, collapsed due to the fundamentally insecure leg supports, thereby presenting Yosef and myself with a technical challenge to restore its stability; a fridge/freezer, which, when not adversely affected by power cuts, is a welcome home for bottles of water and the immense cabbage which has been a mainstay of my diet. The central ceiling light was very dim until it gave up the ghost completely a couple of nights ago. The owner, currently in Addis Ababa, maintains the bulb cannot be replaced; if so, this may represent a design flaw. Until I can find a lamp to buy, I try to remember not to go barefoot in the evenings in a room which has already attracted one large brown scorpion; fortunately, he was rather sleepy, and only waved his tail rather apathetically at me when I encouraged him to leave. The room is generally much admired.

I omitted to mention the further embellishment of the sitting room by a hand-drawn decorated poster proclaiming "Well come father Laurence", a touching gesture by Yosef, who has been very thoughtful and assiduous in helping me settle in ever since I arrived. Given the current hiatus in the water supply, the contents of the plastic water butt in the bathroom lasted barely a day, needed as they were for washing, cooking, washing up and for the extravagance of flushing the "European-style" loo. Yosef efficiently sent a replacement 25 litre plastic can, which arrived by tuk-tuk. I may, however, soon have to join other residents taking their jerry cans to an unappealing metal tank of water which has appeared at the bottom of the road. Once the water is restored, I am looking forward to my first shower, although all the contents of the bathroom are quite likely to get soaked; I must remember to remove them outside before switching on. The bathroom is part-tiled, with some variation where the wall has been excavated and left exposed when fitting the shower. A mirror over the basin is a welcome addition to the basic fittings, despite its collapsed shelf.

The double bedroom is a good size. The bed itself is attractively covered with an Ethiopian-style bedspread to match the curtains and is comfortable enough not to impede a night's sleep; the dilapidated dressing table and matching bedside table, however, provide woefully inadequate storage for a guest intending to stay three months.

The second, single bedroom doubles up as my kitchen. On a relatively stable table of unadorned wood repose my two electric cooking rings. My triumphs so far, thanks to the provisions so thoughtfully pressed upon me before my departure, have been the creation of a superb vegetable omelette, a packet of asparagus soup enhanced by the addition of vegetables, and a very tasty dish of noodles and vegetables. The preparation of these culinary delights is invariably time-consuming, given the time water takes to boil at this altitude, and the constant to-ing and fro-ing to fetch and dispose of water in the bathroom. My trousers and shirts hang above this place of steam and aromas; I have seen fit to remove them each time before they become irretrievably imbued with the smell of dinner. Tomorrow is market day, and Yosef will be taking me to do the week's shopping. He will be keen to see that I am not overcharged, as is customary for all tourists. Meat will be on the shopping list; his advice is to buy meat only on Saturdays when it is fresh. Without cheese to fall back on as an alternative, and no processed meat, I am looking forward to a change from the diet of vegetables and eggs. I might also find an alternative to banana with unbuttered bread for breakfast.

The back door and kitchen window, opening onto the sloping hillside, offer a pleasant view to the distant hills if one overlooks the random piles of breeze blocks which adorn the back garden, or more properly described, yard. I became aware yesterday morning of a procession of small boys, all bearing rocks, coming around the house into the yard and throwing them down in the little remaining space between the breeze blocks. Inquiries elicited a satisfactory response that this was all in order from a youngish man who turned out to be my night watchman. After a scramble over the breeze blocks, a little subsequent rearrangement of the boulders into a mini pyramid permitted me to attach my shirts and underwear to the washing line. Pegs seem to be something of a novelty here; like the packets of soup, noodles and tea, they have eased my domestic management. However, the later retrieval of my washing, by the very inadequate light of my reading torch, was a less happy occasion. Having thoughtlessly pulled the back door fully open, I found I was unable to shut it again because one of the hinges had broken. Alarmed at first, I then reflected that it's a very quiet area, and my guard sleeps to one side of the front entrance, so I wedged the door with the doorstop as best I could and piled up some pots and pans in front of it. Another problem to speak to the landlord about. To cap it all, the phone told me it was low on charge and started buzzing intermittently. I found the charger in the box, but the shape was such that it didn't seem to fit in the adaptor.

I awoke this morning to find no evidence of burglary, but none the less with two lesser problems to solve. Providentially I caught sight of my guard outside (the foreman in the rock-carrying exercise yesterday) and showed him my problematic door. I was grateful that no consideration had to be given to the interior decoration of the area around the door as it was only after the use of considerable force that he found a way to lock the door again. No more opening the door wide in future! Unless, that is, the door is replaced! Later this very morning two men appeared who apparently wanted to deliver a load of prepared timber. Very laborious bringing it all into the house, given the difficult access at the moment, but it seems the doors are to be replaced! Welcome news, except that I don't want a lot of work going on here while I'm in the house.

Having survived the commotion of the timber delivery, it was time to restore my telephonic connection to my local contacts, primarily Yosef and Atinkute, Head of English at my school. I indulged in a tuk-tuk ride up the hill to the shops. After various mystified responses at the sight of my phone charger, eventually one shop assistant took my charger and pulled out the main prong. I could see immediately that it would fit my multi-adapter after all, so went home happy – only to find no phone in my pocket! From relief to despair in a trice, for this was a minor catastrophe.

An hour later, just as I am typing the final part of this letter, despair has turned back to not only relief, but joy and a renewed faith in human nature. Of all unlikely things, the tuk-tuk driver, in whose vehicle I was thinking the phone must have slipped out of my pocket, has just turned up at the house with my phone! It seems that he answered the phone when Yosef rang it, learned that I lived next door to his family home and delivered it back to me. Surely Providence is looking after me!

All in all, not the smoothest of introductions to my sojourn here, but I am certain that I am not the first to discover that a few challenges and privations can be so much better accommodated and endured under a quotidian blue sky and summer temperatures!

Sunday

Today is Sunday. One knows it purely from the silence. I have been out (for me) relatively early, one and half hours after sunrise, partly to survey the scene on this bright morning, partly to investigate water supplies. To the north, the sharp light, cutting through the clarity of the air, thrusts the nearer hills and mountains into sharp profile, the detail of every crag and promontory of the sheer rock face stunningly exposed to the distant viewer. At a lower level the two round, rocky hills of unequal size that dominate the town still look very green, covered by the ubiquitous eucalyptus, cactus and many other trees and shrubs I suspect I shall never identify. Figures wrapped in white can be seen near the top of the hill. The sound of chanting from the churches on the hill, not at first easily distinguishable from the Muslim call to prayer, floats over the town. It is, of course, not a call to prayer - the service began before sunrise and will continue for another hour at least - but no service would be complete without this centuries-old musical accompaniment, whose origin is attributed to the celebrated sixth-century saint Yared. Only the most pious stay for the whole three-hour service, propping themselves up on their prayer sticks inside the dark rock-hewn churches; the remainder perch on the rock surrounding the churches and depart whenever they count their observance completed to their own satisfaction.

Down at street level bougainvillea and poinsettia add colour to the scene. Worshippers wrapped in the traditional white prayer shawl are either returning home already or

Sunday

heading to church singly, in pairs or as a family. The older folk, equipped with fly-whisk, lean on their prayer sticks as they slowly negotiate the hillier and rougher sections of road. The women all cover their head with their shawl, while the men drape the shawl around their shoulders and wear a white turban. But not everybody is so engaged. Three girls take a rest, looking rather miserable, having temporarily laid their burdens of firewood by the road side. In contrast, a few pack-asses clatter freely down the hill, enjoying their current lack of burden. Their owner, striding along behind, greets me cheerily. Yohannes, a young boy who daily asks to clean my shoes, approaches with his winning smile. But today is Sunday; he is not thinking about shoe-shining today. He is dressed in his orange tee-shirt as normal, a contrast to the Sunday worshippers, but claims to have been to church already. He tells me that I can go too; he will show me the way. I am tempted to take up his offer but suddenly feel I would be quite conspicuous in my jumper and safari trousers, and might give offence. I will go another week when I can procure more appropriate clothing.

I return home a different way. I am hailed by three teenage boys who emerge from the shadows of the roadside, munching a snack. They start talking to me, asking me where I am from. This is a daily, and not altogether an unpleasant, occurrence. May they accompany me to practise their English? One in particular speaks English rather well; he tells me his story. He wants to be a guide and would like to go to tourism college next year. Like so many boys here, he has left his family home in the countryside and supports himself here by shoe-shining. His family, he says, doesn't understand that education is the key to (a) life. This takes me back nearly three years, when we heard exactly the same story for the first time. It is hard not to be sympathetic to these ambitious boys who want to break out of an otherwise very limiting environment; the more so because the boys we ourselves agreed to sponsor have done us and themselves proud. But I explain that we can't sponsor any more, and agree, although without offering much hope of success, that I'll try to find him a sponsor on my return home.

In the distance two groups of white-clad men sit on a grassy ridge against a backdrop of hazy mountain ranges. They have been to church, my Grade 10 (Year 11) companion explains to me, and are now enjoying some social time together. I think of the equivalent at St Martin's; coffee at the back of church seems a world away. Being Sunday, these men won't be working, he continues. I think of my tuk-tuk driver friend from the family next-door, who is also observing the day of rest. Regaining my house, I venture forth of necessity with my empty 25 litre plastic water container. On my walk I had seen that a new water tank had arrived on the roadside. Two boys stand impassively watching me as I fill my jerry can and stagger back with it. I suspect

Sunday

that I have just broken a taboo on fetching water on the Sabbath. The boys may, of course, have simply been mute in astonishment that not only was a man performing this menial chore but a white man at that. I am glad to get the water back to my peaceful home. Only the occasional crow of a cock and the call of children interrupt the birdsong outside.

....
....
....

This afternoon I was invited to coffee. Sunday morning after church or mid-afternoon on Sunday are the conventional times for the Ethiopian coffee ceremony. Arriving punctually at the house of my young teacher friend, I follow him through a courtyard where women are engaged in sifting millet on the dry mud and rock floor. We exchange the "Selam" greeting with a polite smile and bow of the head. They are curious; I feel their eyes following me as I step up into my friend's doorway. My eyes have to adjust to the darkness of a windowless room, but before I can discern much at all, a young boy is at my feet demanding attention. I am introduced to the son and heir before even to my hostess, the wife and mother. She is sitting to the right of the doorway behind an array of handleless cups next to her charcoal burner, on which the beans will have been roasted before being ground by hand. The black, oriental-looking coffee pot with its rounded bottom sits ready on its woven ring. Completing the picture, dried grass is spread on the floor before the coffee cups.

I am invited to sit on a stool behind a small wooden table. To my right a cabinet of dark wood provides not only a repository for household items, both treasures and necessities, but also a surface for a small, antique television which continues to flash its images throughout my visit. Unfortunately, my friend's wife has no English, so she stays largely in the background, disappearing once or twice to her left behind a curtain which must conceal the bedroom, while conversation revolves around my experiences in Lalibela so far. My teacher friend considers himself lucky to have found this accommodation to rent. He earns about £1 day (difficult to estimate the equivalent value in our country in terms of buying power, but this would appear to be enough to raise a family but little more). Soon his wife reappears, bearing a large, round dish with a selection of colourful foods invitingly arranged over the injera base. This is a surprise, exceeding the standard hospitality of the coffee ceremony. Water is poured over my hands, and we share the dish. I still find it difficult to observe the custom of eating only with my right hand, so make rather a hash of it. At the end of the meal I am the only one who needs more water to clean his fingers.

Incense from the charcoal burner fills the small room as the dish is taken away. The coffee ceremony has begun. The elegant pot is tilted, and Ethiopia's gift to the

Sunday

world pours forth, rich and black. I am offered sugar, an especially generous gesture, since sugar seems to be difficult to come by here, and is in any case expensive. Coffee is taken with popcorn. The contrast with the mega-helpings I see at the Odeon cinema is stark. I am anxious to abide by the ceremony's convention: after the third little cup has been gratefully accepted and dispatched, it is time to take one's leave. The carefully learnt phrase "Thank you for your hospitality" somehow comes out all wrong, and I leave less than gracefully.

It is now evening. My watch, set to Ethiopian time, shows 12 o'clock - the end of daylight hours. On the horizon the sun sets, a magnificent disc of intense orange. Very soon there is a band of very bright gold all along the most distant mountain range, defying the advancing dark blue. But not for long; the fierce gold band loses its definition and turns to a redder glow. The whole mountain range looks as if it is on fire. But night, of course, extinguishes the conflagration, and very soon parades her own splendour in the heavens. It is always a privilege to marvel at so clear and full a sky at this altitude. Tonight, embellished, but not outshone, by just a sliver of new moon, myriad stars are a forceful reminder to all who live here of the immensity and grandeur of God's creation.

Around me, the nightly orchestra of crickets has struck up. Time to retire inside and treasure these memories.

My Schools

Abyssinia Revisited: Letters from Lalibela

I have now completed three weeks at the two schools in which, due to visa restrictions, I am working illegally. The schools seem very laid-back about the prohibition of any sort of voluntary work by anyone here on a tourist visa; in this small town I suspect they are confident they can iron out any local difficulties with the police, most of whom are probably former pupils.

On my first morning I headed in the same direction as a couple of groups of pupils in light blue uniforms (loose fitting garments: jacket and long skirt for girls, and jacket and trousers for boys, many of whom just pull them on over their jeans) up the cobbled road under the mountain face which looms overhead. Turning off the road onto a dusty footpath, I was pleased to take the picturesque cross-country short cut; however, I didn't allow for the fact that goats and goatherds are no respecters of gradients, and I was soon panting for breath on the ascents. Worse was to follow, for at the depth of the descent into the gorge a particularly steep and dirt-strewn section of the path caused me to slip, spilling my books (and any authority I hoped to exude) into the dust. I was helped to my feet by a small group of girls, who, decorously concealing their amusement, patted the dust off the black trousers I had considered suitable to lend me an air of professionalism. Black is not the colour to wear to school, as I quickly found out, when the dust from the path later became overlaid with a coating of soft school chalk, rendering the appearance of my lower half uncomfortably Chaplinesque.

My Schools

The secondary school is named after St Lalibela, the local king who was responsible for putting this place on the map of Orthodox Christendom; it was he who was inspired at the turn of the twelfth century to order the construction of ten churches, eventually extended to eleven, cut down into the rock, to establish a place of pilgrimage safe from the attentions of marauding militant Muslims. Today his legacy lives on, not only in the annual pilgrimages at Christmas, Epiphany and Easter, but in the school named after him. There is scarcely a pupil who does not sport a wooden or metal cross round his or her neck. One hopes that the king, elevated to sainthood in the 15th century, would show graciousness towards those who don't; the very few girls in Muslim headscarves largely comprise the exceptions.

The secondary school site is sizeable, benefits from charitable help from Millfield School, who appear to send here their out-dated computers, and is at first sight bare of pleasant features. In fact, though, once through the initial barrier of the first block of classrooms one finds an avenue of trees planted between the two lines of classrooms. The teaching staff benefit from their own little green area around the administration block. The smaller preparatory school (for preparatory school read sixth form college) presents an altogether more cared-for appearance, despite a paucity of facilities inside. The approach to the teaching blocks is made through no fewer than four carefully watered, roped off flowerbeds, with similar ones parallel to the classrooms – except that on closer inspection it is not flowers but wild grass that is being tended under trees and shrubs. But these oases of green, contrasting with the dusty surroundings, certainly offer a lesson in determined aspiration. Nearby is a large trough equipped with half a dozen taps which stands thoughtfully high enough for pupils to wash not only their hands but also their hair, although soap and shampoo appear to be in short supply. Sometimes the surprise of a wet head is bestowed on an unsuspecting bystander; teenagers will be teenagers everywhere.

Teaching in both schools is arranged in two shifts to accommodate the discrepancy between the numbers on the school roll and the number of classrooms. The day begins in front of two flagpoles with an assembly of all morning pupils (some of whom are literally lightly whipped into line), who sing the national anthem as the national and regional flags are hoisted. Every opportunity is taken to try to instil a sense of nationhood among this motley combination of so many different peoples, cultures and languages. However, watching from a distance of less than fifty yards, I was by the end still none the wiser as to the melody of this anthem, such was the enthusiasm with which it was rendered.

The pupils then disperse into the rows of one-storey classroom blocks. Despite the precision with which the lessons are timetabled – each one in theory exactly forty-two minutes in length – it seems that observance of the schedule is fairly optional. This throws lesson-planning into disarray. The disinclination of many pupils to carry to school the relevant textbooks for the day's lessons is another disruptive factor. I think the maximum number of books I have had in a class of about forty is six; the minimum was one. Nobody seems to have a school bag, and lockers would be an unaffordable expense for the school. Flexibility is, here more than anywhere, the order of the day. Sometimes it is possible to proceed with groups of up to ten trying to share one book, sometimes it is better to abandon the textbook altogether and resort to chalk and talk. The blackboard fixed to the wall is the one feature alleviating the otherwise unadorned painted walls. Any competing distraction is of an aural nature; whenever the adjoining lesson involves some sort of audio-visual aid, the commentary booms through the wall, rendering concentration and communication twice as difficult as usual. Who would choose to process thoughts in a foreign tongue when he can listen with no effort at all to a presentation on the internal organs of the monkey? Perhaps the subject of HIV-AIDS and how to repel unwanted advances will command a more focussed attention. Looking ahead in my textbook for pupils in their final year, I see with trepidation that I shall have to become an overnight authority on this topic. Even if I cannot claim any reliable knowledge regarding this particular subject, at least I shall be the only one in the room who understands the text. What is authority half the time if not bluff?

Spread in random fashion throughout a room of dust and strewn paper, sitting at old-fashioned school desks designed for two but here usually seating at least three, pupils are like teenagers in any school anywhere: a mix of the more confident and outgoing and the timid - roughly in a proportion of 1:8. Girls fall, regrettably but not unexpectedly, largely into the latter category, which no doubt partly explains the government's policy of positive discrimination in assigning places to girls in higher education. I will persevere with my efforts to coax the shy majority into speech. The occasional reward of a pen for active participation might eventually produce results; the lure of a coveted object should never be under-estimated. However, even when emboldened into volunteering an answer, the boy or girl usually, embarrassingly, has to repeat his or her contribution at least twice for me, since pronunciation of English is no less a challenge for them than Amharic with its clunky fricatives is for me. The staff, as might be expected, are more fluent and confident, and speak enough English to make conversation very difficult. (That *bon mot* is lifted straight from Evelyn Waugh, I have to admit; impossible to put it better.)

Their staff room is austere indeed. To the wall is affixed the odd scrappy timetable. A few random tubular benches with plywood backs and seats, some furnished with partially excavated foam cushions, are the only physical comfort offered. Blandishments of a better life are broadcast unceasingly on the most ancient television I have seen in fifty years; as in most Ethiopian establishments and homes, life without a constantly distracting television screen is apparently unthinkable. For the time being, the most they can aspire to is to be champion table tennis player; the table in front of the staff room is constantly the scene of closely-fought duels.

Last Thursday my afternoon lessons at the secondary school were cancelled, though nobody thought to tell me officially. I learned that it was the annual day for celebrating the nation, and upon mentioning this to the school authorities promptly received an invitation to be a guest at the festivities to be staged by the pupils. I arrived fifteen minutes before the event was scheduled to begin; thirty minutes later an announcement was made over the loudspeaker, but it did not herald anything in particular. By this time I had been given a seat of honour, in the shade next to the panel of judges – for this, I learned, was to be a competitive presentation by diverse groups – and in direct line of fire from a loudspeaker which blasted popular music into my very quickly deafened right ear. The mood was indeed festive. Before me was a notional arena in which the performances were to be presented, pupils happily pressing forward around the circumference in eager anticipation; some more enterprising ones had scaled trees; rather too many latecomers had scaled a nearby outbuilding and were about to precipitate its collapse. Overhead flew the flags of the nation whose undeniable diversity and theoretical unity we were celebrating; the whole delightful scene was set off by the backdrop of towering cliffs and circling vultures. And at last the entertainment began.

I don't think I have enjoyed a school production so much for a long time. The schedule began with a short morality tale, acted out by three older pupils; its message was to urge all young Ethiopians to devote themselves to building up their country. It was reminiscent of the Soviet era, but with a lot more jollity; the crowd laughed at the funny bits and were inspired to applaud and cheer at the uplifting denouement. Next came a string of individuals dressed not in the different regional costumes but as representatives of the professions, trades and crafts which were going to be necessary for the future prosperity of the country – anything from doctor to roadbuilder. These worthy heralds of a stirring future then broke into an exhilarating series of dances in which individuals showed off their skills at shoulder-dancing, hip-shaking and foot-stamping, while the remainder, chorus-line-like, continued to provide a deftly agile backing group. In an order which I cannot precisely remember there followed karate practitioners, the oldest of whom looked so aggressive in their moves

My Schools

towards one another that I expected a serious casualty any moment, but amazingly the punches and kicks always stopped fractionally short of their target; poets of all ages and sizes, some of whom were sufficiently witty, or possibly risqué or defamatory, to delight the crowd, all of whom were roundly applauded; a "Top of the Form" quiz show, in which four selected representatives of different classes competed at two desks placed mid-arena to show off their knowledge about Ethiopia; solo singers who would each have excelled on "Ethiopia's Got Talent", especially the older boy who was awarded a round nought by the judges; a gravity-defying team of rubbery gymnasts, whose act climaxed in the elevation of one younger member to stand, hands free, high up on top of a human pyramid. The boy survived – this time.

By now the arena had markedly shrunk in size. The enthusiasm of the crowd, pressing forward, had left the teaching staff and older pupils no option but to wield sticks between acts to drive the revellers back. The longer the show continued, the greater the number of staff who were engaged in physically restoring order. Everybody seemed to enjoy this part of the proceedings as much as the performances; smiles quickly re-emerged on all faces. The flailing arms and batons reached a climactic kerfuffle, to which a recently arrived young policeman dutifully and enthusiastically contributed, so that on one side of the arena the spectators disappeared briefly in a swirling dust storm. The headmaster continued to smile serenely throughout, an admirable exemplar of keeping calm and carrying on; after all, no boy had fallen out of a tree; no skulls had been cracked; and the outbuilding had not collapsed. Clearly a wonderful afternoon had been had by all.

The next day it was back to white lab-technician-style coats (called gowns), chalk and talk, and disgruntled teachers bemoaning the lack of motivation on the part of so many pupils and dreaming of escaping to something better. This is a language I recognise! Lalibela is becoming more of a home from home every day....

Circus Lalibela
Children's Security
Reproductive
Anti HIV-AIDS &
Art Association

Tel 0910144206
0927471409
0920477701

Village Life

Abyssinia Revisited: Letters from Lalibela

I've implied in the title of this letter that Lalibela is a village, although it is, properly speaking, a town. It even has its own airport. But it is only in the last twenty years that this "legendarily inaccessible" fastness in the Northern Highlands (Philip Briggs in the excellent Bradt Guide) has morphed into a most unlikely town on the mountainside, extending its tentacles in all directions, wherever the rocky surface can be sufficiently levelled to build on. The road constructed to connect Lalibela with its airport is being upgraded and is receiving an asphalt surface, thanks to Chinese engineers and Ethiopian labour; the principal streets of the town have over the last two years been equipped with street lights and laid with cobblestones, so that tuk-tuks now ply their trade as happily and usefully as in Delhi; hotels have mushroomed as Lalibela has been promoted as the number one tourist destination in Ethiopia; innumerable small cafes and bars line the roads, each manned by a lady proprietor (and her sisters and her cousins and her aunts), alongside shacks selling all of life's necessities: groceries, hardware, clothing. But it still feels like a big village.

Perhaps this is because the standard form of locomotion is Shank's pony. Nobody feels the need to walk on the pavement, even if there is one; the tuk-tuks and the odd minibus may hoot, but more to warn of their approach rather than to shoo pedestrians off the road. Donkeys, or rather donkey drivers, will not

Village Life

be surrendering their prior claim to road space in the foreseeable future - a sort of agrarian equivalent of sail before steam. The variety of people and dress to be seen on the roads is a continual delight. Ladies adorned in bright headscarves wearing ankle-length dresses of colourful light-weight material that billow lightly in any breeze, strolling under umbrellas of all colours; other women, some young, some of indeterminate age, carrying burdens in the traditional manner resting on their rump at the base of their spine, so that over time it is not surprising that they walk at a corrupted perpendicular; others carry babies higher on their back, wrapped in their shawl; a few younger women dare to invite disapproval in their tight jumper and trousers; older men in white turbans and enveloped in shawls lean on their staff as they shuffle along; woolly-hatted men draped in a thicker blanket, in from the countryside, stride purposefully toward the centre, their staff held firmly across their shoulders, for the moment devoid of a heavy sack or a sheep; young men in bright tee-shirt and jeans, with hairstyles that range from neatly shorn black curls through fuzzy-wuzzy to something that would excite a would-be rapper; school pupils of all ages in their uniforms of dark red or light blue, envious perhaps of the smarter dark blue waistcoat and white shirt of the sixth-formers; hopeful shoe-shiners of school age and beyond with their little boxes and routine of clapping the brush smartly against the side of the box whenever they want the client to change feet; and everywhere at every hour of the day children, even the youngest of whom are fully rehearsed in crying "Hallo. Welcome to Lalibela", often enough with the sequel "Pen?"

There is a freedom in the air here. The roads of Lalibela are still a playground for children, reminiscent of the streets of my childhood. The lack of traffic means even the smallest have the freedom of the street to walk to school; groups of them are everywhere, chatting, playing games in the road, bowling a hoop, occasionally squabbling; nobody bars them from investigating the novelty of the roadworks, a natural adventure playground. Last week I saw an open-back truck turn out of the gates of the preparatory school with pupils happily standing in the back and sitting on the sides, an unquestioned normality for them all. This freedom from constraint and regulation may, of course, lead to accidents, the consequences of which cannot be belittled; but it seems also to release energy, a means to unimpeded self-fulfilment, a "can-do" outlook.

Although I have seen no sign of it, I am told that chewing khat is one of those unrestricted, albeit discouraged, social occupations for some younger men. Equally absent from public view are cigarettes; maybe they just can't afford to smoke. Strangely enough, one of the few social prohibitions, that of any homosexual activity, has an unexpectedly liberating effect. Although occasionally a young male and female couple, or a couple of girls, can be observed holding hands, it is the number of men and boys of all ages holding hands, or with arms around one another's necks or waists, that is striking. Growing up, and sleeping, in close physical proximity to one another, they obviously never consider it necessary or desirable to restrict the outward show of natural affection for one another, enjoying a freedom which the law paradoxically indirectly protects and promotes. Respect is certainly paid to the elderly, in language and in behaviour, but in a country where it is normal to know and address everyone by his or her first name there can be no stuffiness; perhaps it is a sense of mutual dependence in these communities which fosters open and affectionate relations as the social norm.

As the weeks have passed, I am now more often than not greeted in the area where I live and around the schools with "Hallo teacherrr!" (When conversation becomes animated, the insistent trill of the Amharic R recalls an aviary of excited budgerigars.) Even the older non-English speakers nod their head and salute me with a respectful Amharic equivalent: *gashe* - an irony if ever there was one, since it literally means "my shield" and yet I have never been so dependent as here on the goodwill of others. The shopkeepers know me now too; the tourist souvenir shops have given up trying to entice me in; after an early, stern word from Yosef in one case, I am no longer charged the tourist price for everyday goods. The only building where it is an advantage to be obviously non-native is the bank, where I am spared the frisking by the military guard outside. The little lock-ups in my vicinity are staffed by anyone from a granny to a child. Why should this cause surprise in a country where a four or five-year-old can be in sole charge of driving sheep or goats along the road?

My butcher's shop deserves a special mention; it is definitely a step up from the usual corrugated metal shack. The square structure of eucalyptus is capped with a traditional conical thatched roof; service is through a hatch hung with eucalyptus leaves, which look very attractive but singularly fail in their purpose of protecting the carcases hanging behind from the incursion of flies. A table and chairs are set out in front of this picturesque little shop on a floor of strewn dried grass, although apart from beef tartare I am not sure what would-be customers might expect to be served here. Purchasing meat is without any of the agonies of choice at home; there is beef or beef; Ethiopians do not eat pork, and mutton or goat is apparently hard to come by except on feast days.

The true joy of shopping in Lalibela can, however, only be experienced on market day. Radiating from the centre there is a whirl of activity, in the manner of a true market town. The market is held, fully open to the sun, on a promontory with views to the distant mountains. The scene from afar is as colourful as any in

Village Life

Africa, I am sure. To the right, as I start out, a densely packed assembly of awnings of every hue, shape and size confronts me in the distance; to the left is the more open area where donkeys, sheep, goats and oxen are tethered. Although by now trading has been underway for some time, by the third hour of the day there are still small processions of animals being driven towards the market, some along the precipitous footpath which is my most direct approach. Momentarily distracted by two colourful birds delighting in the luxuriant vegetation of one of the two stream beds which the path traverses, I have to step aside to allow the passage of the Saturday regulars: boys steadying on their heads baskets piled high or sacks bulging at the seams; groups of ladies, each holding an umbrella, surprisingly sure-footed on the rough ground; a laden donkey being driven by a turbaned, blanketed countryman. There is a short pause in the procession as the donkey is cajoled to ascend a twelve-foot cleft in the rock, comparable to a scramble on any one of the more demanding Lake District paths. The reluctant beast manages the challenge, but only with physical encouragement. The procession resumes, umbrellas on the way up giving way, in places, to umbrellas coming down.

We reach the market. To the left a few people are taking advantage of the shade cast by a solitary acacia tree on the edge of the escarpment; to the right, shaded by umbrellas or makeshift shelters, vendors squat on the ground, as far as the eye can see. In a surprising display of organisation each area seems to be dedicated to a certain type of produce. I come at first to poultry, the scrawny but biddable chickens clutched impassively by their owners. Of more interest to me are their eggs, carefully presented in baskets of straw. Before buying a single one, Yosef picks each up, puts it to his ear and shakes it. Should I emulate this when next in Waitrose? Payment is made in filthy low-value notes. Next come potatoes, then cabbage, spinach, tomatoes, red peppers, garlic, huge piles of red onions, all set out on the ground. I get adventurous and buy some chilli. The displays of fruit are tempting, although hardly in the pristine condition of the supermarket at home: oranges, lemons, bananas, papaya, mango, and a small round fruit with pinkish flesh and lots of small pips whose identity I have not yet established. Should one pick the greener fruit or the yellower? The passageways between the serried ranks of vendors are very narrow. Progress is slow. The occasional donkey noses its way between the displays. The air is suffused with dust; most people are coughing. Yosef frequently stops to give the Ethiopian shoulder-to-shoulder greeting to his acquaintances; he seems to know half the population. Even I am hailed: "Hallo teacherrr! How arrre you?".

We ignore the clothing and grain sections and head for the honey department. Home-made honey is a feature

Village Life

of the market. The local country people vie with one another for custom; we inspect their big tin containers. Most are busy stirring their mixture. I am surprised to see a coarse dark yellow/orange glutinous substance. This is red honey, I am told, a honey product with medicinal value; for which ailment I am not told - maybe it's for dust-filled lungs? - for by this time we have moved on to a man wrapped in a blanket , seated, as all the others are, on the ground, stirring what looks like honey of a very good, rich colour. First we have to buy a plastic pot. We lift the lid of our pot while the vendor receives a cursory hand wash from his companion and proceeds to plunge the notionally cleansed hand into the tin container of honey. A handful is scooped out and transferred into my pot, and then the operation is repeated until the agreed level is reached. I confess my heart sinks a little at the sanitary implications of this method of serving up my honey.

A demented tuk-tuk driver tries to force his way through the rows of vendors but does not prevail, becoming embroiled in what here might be termed a traffic honey. Having breathed in enough dust for one morning, I make my way out of this dense whorl of humanity and head for home with my purchases. Casting caution to the wind, I discover the unique, rich, sweet flavour of home-made Lalibelan honey. What is more, I am the joyful possessor of a genuine honey pot. Eat your heart out, Pooh bear!

My Gregorian Christmas

Abyssinia Revisited: Letters from Lalibela

I had originally thought this letter would be entitled 'My Christmases', but a limited imagination had to yield to an unexpected wealth of experience, hence the revised focus on only one Christmas at a time. Few people are accorded the privilege of experiencing two Christmases within a fortnight; I suspect that most are only too pleased that they are not. But strip away Father Christmas, the muzak, the buying frenzy and the largely alcohol-fuelled Christmas spirit, and, above all, the pressure to come up to everybody else's expectations, and the central joy of Christmas is a delight and privilege that more than bears repetition.

My first Christmas began in a manner quite unforeseen. I received a last-minute invitation from the staff of a nearby hotel to join them and their Western guests for a special evening celebration to mark Christmas Eve. I arrived to find the lights in the round, tukul-style restaurant dimmed; in fact, it was lit largely by candlelight. Lanterns had been placed on the bar to illuminate a few reindeer galloping through tinsel towards an advent wreath, and more were laid out on the floor to delineate an area dedicated to the coffee ceremony that was to be the centrepiece of the evening's events. This was an extravagant version of the usual, more modest array of charcoal burner, coffee pot and cups. Incense wafted through the air, in its anticipation of the arrival of the three wise men perhaps a little premature; integral, though, to the ceremony. A carol greeted the ears; a laptop was treating us to an unfortunate American rendering of 'The First Noel'. I expect it helped the other guests feel at home, by and large Americans who had temporarily escaped from their host Middle Eastern countries. It was doubtless well-meant.

A large Jamaican-born lady, inspired by the crooning coming from the laptop, thought we should contribute to the carol-singing, but, since she herself professed an inability to sing, this seed of an idea fell on stony ground. As the first cup of coffee was handed round, a rival beverage made its appearance: the honey wine of local repute; at first sip, beautifully smooth and sweet; after many such sips, fatal to any pretence to dignity. A cake was produced. 'Merry Christmas', piped in some sort of red cream onto a shallow rectangular base, was just legible in the dim light; bananas flanked the sides, while flowers completed the decoration around the perimeter. The cake was acclaimed. There followed a moment or two of quiet as all present kept to themselves their thoughts about the unusual consistency of this apparently sugarless, eggless, injera-style baking.

By now raki was being offered; the music had moved on to Ethiopian dance music; one or two of the younger Americans were persuaded to venture onto their feet to try to emulate the neck-breaking, shoulder-dislocating moves of the traditional dance, the *askista*, performed with gusto by the invariably smiling waiter, Tare, who proved to be as good a dancer as he is a restaurant host. Inevitably there was some curiosity as to what I was doing here. One American teacher of English, at present happy enough in Japan, pronounced himself inspired to follow suit; after forty years of classroom graft, the prospect of being applauded at the end of a lesson evidently has its attractions.

By the third hour after sunset (the equivalent of 9 pm) guests were taking their leave. Early to bed and early to rise is the norm here - leading to some evidence of health and wisdom perhaps, but not much sign of wealth. Back home I found the CD I had brought with me for Christmas; it began with 'Silent Night', sung in German by the Vienna Boys Choir. I opened the door and took the laptop outside under the vast, silent, starlit sky. Right on cue, a shooting star briefly conjured up a pale imitation of the guiding star of old. The soft, simple melody and harmonies of 'Stille Nacht, Heilige Nacht' had never seemed more moving.

The next morning the waitress from the hotel (who doubles as the accountant) was to accompany me to church. Conscious of the need to be ready on time for the early start, I set the alarm clock that night for the twelfth hour. I need not have. About fifteen minutes before my elected time to surface I was rudely awoken, as I had been every previous Sunday morning - but had forgotten - by what sounded like a car alarm disturbing the peace and quiet for about thirty seconds before it gave way to a hoarse voice proclaiming some message, urgently, insistently, repetitively. It was the equivalent of our bells, calling us to church. Fortified only by a cup of tea, I drew some curious looks as I waited at the first hour outside my house, my upper body enveloped in the white prayer shawl I had been lent. Although of thin material, over my bare arms it made a difference at this time of day. Arsema came into view, accompanied by the Jamaican lady who had wanted to sing carols the night before. She too had acquired from somewhere the obligatory shawl to cover her head and shoulders. Progress was slow, but the talk was as entertaining as it was instructive. The lady had been a preacher in a Pentecostal church but was now a Roman Catholic; she could not abide the thought of not going to church on Christmas Day. A good number of other churchgoers were before us and behind us, toiling up the hill, oblivious of the fact that it was Christmas Day for the tiny minority of visitors.

We arrived at a passageway cut deep into the rock; it was the entrance to the church of St Michael. We were far too late to find room within. Climbing up the hillside of smooth, bare red rock, we joined the hundreds of worshippers who were also 'locked out'. They were mostly standing looking at the rooftop of the church, which for us was at ground level, from where emanated an incessant chanting. I noticed, clambering about high on rocks to the right, three or four Westerners armed with cameras. One was pointed intently at the proceedings down in the trench outside the church. A wave of disapproval passed through me at their incongruous appearance and the insensitivity of their actions. Then I remembered that I too had been only too keen to photograph the proceedings of the Epiphany service three years ago. This time, however, I felt I was a participant, not an onlooker. I tried to concentrate on events. The Jamaican lady was much moved by the presence of God. Unfortunately, the presence of God seemed to be insufficient as a focus for worship; her commentary continued unabated until we heard bells being struck and the congregation stirred themselves to kneel on the rocky ground. It was the consecration of the Host. They also believe in transubstantiation, murmured my garrulous companion, obviously comforted by this thought as she lowered herself with difficulty onto the rock. From the kneeling position, the devout inclined their heads forward to touch the rock as they prayed.

After the passage of some time, the crowd turned away from the church. The solo chanting had now changed to choral chanting to a symphony of solemn drumbeats. Disengaging myself from the small group of children who had encircled my companion, I turned to see that a large natural bowl in the rock to our left was now filling with white-clad worshippers; their attention was directed to a man standing on a rock at the base of a central tree, the upper half of which was stripped bare and pointed starkly to the blue heavens. The preacher was dressed in a golden robe, overlaid with a dark red vestment. He held a bible in his left hand. The sight caused me to recall the stone base I had seen at Corinth, where St Paul had reputedly preached in the open to the citizenry; except that any conversions to the faith today were unlikely; these were not unbelievers. On the contrary: during the forty-minute sermon, delivered without notes, members of the congregation queued quietly to be healed and blessed by colourfully dressed deacons who passed an ornately carved wooden hand-cross over the torso of the believer, in much the same way as a security officer sweeps the long-suffering passenger with his electronic metal detector at Heathrow airport. Although the motive may be different, a similarly reassuring effect is achieved, in this case more comforting perhaps to both body and soul. I have yet to observe the final act of gratefully kissing the hand-cross transferred to a metal detector at Heathrow.

Upturned festive umbrellas of gold and scarlet brocade were now to be seen above the heads of the congregation: the equivalent of the collection plate. Notes were tossed in as the deacons moved through the crowd. Rather more fun than at home. Finally, the moment my companion had been waiting for: the arrival of the communion bread, piled high in large flabby, hand-torn chunks on wide, flat baskets. With commendable ecumenism, she had already received healing and a blessing. Proclaiming that she wanted a part of anything blessed, she dispatched a couple of her young coterie to collect some of the holy bread. On their return they thrust a piece into my hand too; as I suspected, yet another variation on injera. I swallowed piece by piece the soft, chewy, spongy substance, together with my scruples as to whether, as a non-Orthodox believer, I was entitled to this sacrament. But perhaps the Jamaican-born lady from Texas, now teaching in Kuwait, had a point: God's blessing is for all, no matter how it is delivered. And particularly on this day.

The service was at an end. The preacher stepped down from his natural pulpit; the crowds headed for the rocky descent to the road. I tried again to remind myself that this was Christmas Day. The blue sky and warm sun shone on the flood of white-clad faithful returning to their homes. I thanked Arsema for accompanying us to the service and deviated to have my shoes shined; one boy at least would be able to buy something to eat this Christmas Day. The last I saw of my unlikely Christmas morning companion was of a slow-moving figure in the distance, still surrounded by children.

Arrived back home, I made to unpack the card and present I had been given by Belinda to bring out with me. Risking the absurd incongruity, I put 'O Tannenbaum' into the CD player. A mistake. As the deeply affecting, nostalgic melody filled the room and I looked at the card of a Christmas tree and a blazing fire, read the loving words and opened the packet of Christmas goodies, I was in an instant transported back to our traditional family Christmas Day. I was momentarily overcome by an overwhelming pang of homesickness. It took me by surprise.

However, a quick recovery was required, for I had a sixth-former coming for an individual lesson in a few minutes. Prising a chocolate coin out its gold foil wrapping, I realised that, apart from the trickle of precious honey on a piece of bread, this was the breaking of an unintentional fast; for a whole month I had consumed no sweet confectionery. It was a moment to savour. My Christmas Day would continue in its novel way. I had a celebratory restaurant meal to look forward to, followed by an invitation to a coffee ceremony, and the extravagance and delight of a phone call from home. But the best was to come later: an individual Christmas pudding with custard! And, of course, within a few days a second Christmas....

My Orthodox Christmas

Christmas is coming: out of the sunshine, with two days to go, there's a slight chill in the air, and the nights are very cold. The goose is getting fat: for goose substitute goat; one such, recently arrived in a neighbour's backyard, in his displeasure, and possible apprehension, is drowning out the nearby crying baby and the crowing cockerels; doubtless very shortly to fall silent. Please put a penny in the old man's hat: please put a birr in the old pilgrim's hand.

The pilgrims started arriving a good week before Christmas. Unmistakable in their little processions, looking tired and dirty in their blankets and turbans, they tramp along through the dust; the men bear their bundles on sticks, the women carry their bundles on their backs, wrapped in their shawl; some are barefoot. Their once handsome Ethiopian faces, now prematurely aged, with skin deeply creased or tightly stretched, bear all the hallmarks of a hard life. They are welcomed to their destination at specially erected shelters decorated with bunting. Music, of a religious nature, I'm informed, gives way occasionally to what are obviously bible readings; in large letters on the canvas behind the rows of chairs, in both Amharic and English, the text of John 13:15 defining Christian obligation: "You should do as I have done to you". And so volunteers, mainly older boys and younger men, invite the newly-arrived to seat themselves in front of a bowl of water; a meal of injera and shiro is put into their hands while the volunteers

My Orthodox Christmas

wash their dirty feet. It is a scene that could have taken place two thousand years ago.

As the numbers have increased over recent days, figures swathed in white have become a constant addition to the scenery around the churches. Many are to be found restoring themselves at the holy spring next to the site of St George's church. Very many are camped out in the cleared area between the old two-storey stone tukuls unique to Lalibela. The more pecunious arrive in dirty buses, which, plastered with crosses proclaiming God's love for his world, expel foul fumes into the otherwise pure mountain air. Some of these more fortunate pilgrims have arranged rented accommodation; others are shown into the schools, whose classrooms, allegedly cleaned of dust and torn paper, will become their home for the duration of the festivities.

Traders have arrived in prodigious numbers; the market is also functioning every day just now. In fact, the market has enveloped the town; crowds fill the streets, which are festooned with bunting and are lined by traders offering souvenir Lalibela tee-shirts and crosses alongside Hollywood-style sunglasses. In the centre of the street young men in green bibs act as traffic policemen; waving canes, they direct the biddable pedestrians to keep left; tuk-tuks no longer ply the streets for trade, their licence temporarily suspended. Commerce may appear to have upstaged the religious festival – perhaps it was ever thus – but the music, the announcements and, for the pilgrim visitors, the roadside refreshments suggest otherwise. Smoke from the charcoal burners and steam from the kettles temporarily replace the suggestion of dust in the nostrils. As we advance through the crowd, we glimpse a densely packed gathering in Holy Cross Square; the adherents of the group, inevitably all dressed in white, kneel and then, rising again, proceed to parade in a circle; rows of onlookers, also in white, are sitting on the stone terracing overlooking the road; it is a bereavement gathering, Yosef tells me. Tethered in a row, mules, which have brought many of the assembled, stand quietly by, glad of a break.

These mules are only a short distance from where their fellow creatures are experiencing a far more exciting day. The market is today primarily a livestock market. "Seething" would be an understatement, although Yosef promises even denser crowds tomorrow, when food produce will be as much in evidence as animals are today: rows and rows of mules, donkeys, and, a new sight for me in Lalibela, horses. I move gingerly along the narrow path behind them, wary of a back-kick at any moment. Tightly packed together, the animals are examined critically by would-be purchasers. Some need to test the horses. The crowd is forced to part as an uninhibited rider spurs his horse through the throng. Taking avoiding action, I have to guard against tripping over a countryman's staff; against overturning a hobbling three-legged sheep being led by one tied foreleg; even more critically against stumbling onto the fiendish horns of an ox.

We come upon the goats and sheep. Yosef and I feel the flanks of a few goats, interested as we are in purchasing one for his family's Christmas feast. Unsurprisingly, many seem thin; the meatier-looking specimens, we soon discover, command a price in excess of our budget. We eventually give up; Yosef will leave this to a cousin who is in the country, where prices might be lower.

We continue to make our way through the bedlam, avoiding treading in animal dung where we can. More of a hazard is the prevalence of sticks, none of them, mercifully, pointed, but enough to cause damage to an unwary eye: countrymen shouldering sticks, animal drivers waving sticks, priests and pilgrims bearing sticks topped by a metal cross; other pilgrims pushing forward with prayer sticks; traders carrying bundles of these across their shoulders; even the few graceful ladies wielding umbrellas pose a risk here. Extricating ourselves intact from the throng, on the far side I am struck by the sight of a rider astride a horse: a magnificent man in traditional white blanket and half-turban, displaying excellent horsemanship. This, surely, is a sight that has not changed one jot since Evelyn Waugh's travels in Abyssinia in the thirties.

Abyssinia Revisited: Letters from Lalibela

On Christmas Eve I escape temporarily from the magnet pull of Lalibela. We drive along the High Street, or rather we inch our way through a commotion of buses, minibuses, 4x4s and trucks, the density of which recalls Oxford Street as it used to be in December, all the while avoiding the pedestrians to whom the streets primarily belong at this time. We descend the steep winding dirt road which leads out into the countryside; the flat valley floor lies before us, the next range of mountains beyond; along the road still more groups of men walk to market. In hillier country again, the parched trees are stunted, unless next to one of the few mountain streams which flow languidly at this time of year through the occasional deep, rocky channels. We jolt our way past some signs of human life amid the arid hills: figures walk singly or in pairs in what appear to be the most desolate places; here and there three or four round, thatched tukuls shelter behind the family stockade; the occasional small village sits on the crown of a lower conical hill; hardy peasants, working to nature's unassailable rhythms, have taken the plough to patches of barren, stony land; areas of stubble indicate a harvest of teff, piles of which can be seen drying outside the tukuls. Somehow the resilient inhabitants scratch a living in this wilderness. And then walk to Lalibela to give thanks.

We arrive at the foot of a steep, narrow valley with running water in the stream bed. The blue-tinged leaves of the young eucalyptus provide a pleasant relief from the tired-looking green of the indigenous deciduous trees. Some attempts at terracing suggest crops of beans, lentils and sorghum; the houses are rectangular here, of newer construction; evidence of some prosperity. I quickly discover that this is largely thanks to foreign visitors like me; I am charged double the amount I am expecting before being allowed to climb the well-graded, paved path that leads to our destination: the late eleventh or early twelfth century church of Yemrehanna Kristos.

At the top of this gently ascending staircase, the first impression is disappointing: we are confronted with a wall of breeze blocks below a sheer face of rock. But once we have left our shoes alongside the dozens of other pairs at the foot of the wall; once we have penetrated the narrow entrance and are standing in our stockinged feet on bamboo matting; once we have accustomed our eyes to the comparative gloom of the cavern revealed behind the protective wall, a wonder of a building is before us: in the words of Philip Briggs of the Bradt Guide, a church resembling "a gigantic layered chocolate cream cake"! The church is constructed of alternating horizontal layers of wood and granite faced with white gypsum; the two levels of windows, some of stone and some of wood, are all carved in different designs. The interior boasts a fine central pitched wooden roof with a dome over the east end and horizontal panels to the rear and sides, once again carved to a variety of designs and, in addition, painted; in fact, almost every surface of the interior, whether of stone or wood, displays paintings of either biblical scenes or highly ornate variations on the cross or the star of David. Some of the carving is in every way as intricate and imaginative as anything of comparable age in Europe.

I feel like an intruder in this sanctuary of Orthodoxy. The Mass has only just finished, and there are plenty of pilgrims here: kneeling down at the foot of the exterior walls with head bowed to the ground; kissing the walls and the doorpost before entering; crossing themselves while stepping over the worn stone threshold; kissing the hand cross held by the priests guarding the Holy of Holies. This latter is the repository of the *tabot*, frequently referred to as a replica of the Ark of the Covenant, but which is more accurately a replica of the tablets of stone inscribed with the Ten Commandments. The priests look on impassively as Western tourists, alien to the Church's traditions, size up the objects to be captured on film, take aim with their camera lens, and with Dalek-like insensitivity shoot.

Later, back home, the television is switched on. The Christmas night service in Lalibela has begun in and around the church of St Mary and is being shown live. Rows of priests in white robes enlivened with red, green or gold flashes of colour parade slowly through the clouds of incense, solemnly chanting; lines of deacons

My Orthodox Christmas

in their black cloaks and high white turbans practise their uniform swaying motion, raising their sistra to the right and to the left to some imperceptible rhythm; patriarchs invited from many parts of the country look on, a formidable phalanx of stern church fathers in black.

Despite the good view accorded by the television cameras we repair to the site itself. Who could be in Lalibela on Christmas Eve without being physically part of the service? I find myself in much the same location on the rocks as on Christmas morning two weeks previously. To my surprise, however, I am having to avoid stepping on bodies completely wrapped in white blankets lying prone on the solid rock floor. Having, in many cases, come so far to be present at this celebration, they cannot, it seems, stay awake any longer. We listen for a while to the chanting and the drum accompaniment ascending from the excavated area in front of the barely visible church only a few yards from us. I state my intention to obtain a ticket entitling me to a view another time; I reconsider when Yosef tells me the service lasts twelve hours, and without being in place at least two hours prior to the start one wouldn't see much anyway.

We move on across the rocks, circumnavigating by the light of our torches the sleeping pilgrims, insulated to the best of their ability against the cold of the night. Below us appears to be one gigantic open-air field hospital; bodies wrapped in blankets lie side by side across a vast open area, protected here and there by trees. But not all are comatose: a few groups of younger visitors are singing hymns and clapping to their own rival rhythms; further up the hill patient worshippers queue to gain access to another church from where the first solo chanting emanates as we pass; at the corner volunteers around fires are already preparing to feed the five thousand tomorrow morning. Fish will be on the menu only by divine intervention.

Back to the technological miracle of the television for a visual counterpart to the acoustic experience. By the sixth hour of the night, six hours into the service, I make for my bed, falling asleep without so much as an empathetic thought for the faithful out on the hard, cold rock.

By the twelfth hour, at the break of the new day, I am up again and heading towards the churches once more. By the time I regain my position on the rocks, Mass has been said and the mood of solemnity has already changed; the congregation is excited, in celebratory mood. Now every square inch of the rock surrounding the churches is covered with a sea of white; the more athletic have climbed trees; all eyes are trained on the edge of the deep trench dividing us from the sunken churches. By the first hour, when light has re-established its pre-eminence over darkness, it is to a resounding chorus of ululation that the first priests emerge from

My Orthodox Christmas

the church, bearing a huge picture of the Virgin Mary with the Christ Child against a background of a curtain of silk. They mount the rocky surround, followed by others in a wide variety of ecclesiastical dress, all vying with one another for the prize for the most colourful. An equally impressive picture of the Archangel Gabriel is borne aloft to more ululations. The procession establishes itself precariously on the very edge of the sheer rock wall; with a little imagination the giant festive silken umbrellas carried by the priests could almost be the appurtenances of a troupe of high-wire artists; but they are all sure-footed enough to retain their dignity, and after so many hours still sufficiently compos mentis to lead the happy chanting evidently enjoyed by the congregation. It is, however, the more uniformly dressed deacons in their white robes who follow them onto the precipice that prompt the loudest ululations, the most enthusiastic clapping along to the beat, the noisiest blasts on the bugles; in time they sway and dip, in time they rattle their sistra, and in time at the end of each "number" they bow their heads low towards the church at their feet.

The procession advances very slowly around the perimeter of the hidden church until the sun, rising over the trees, casts its first rays on the complex; the rock reddens; the white sea dazzles; the gold silk in the priests' vestments glistens; the sequins adorning the ceremonial umbrellas flash and glitter. The chanting quickens in pace; the congregation claps ever more enthusiastically in time until the climax is reached.

And suddenly it is over for another year: Christmas Day has dawned; joy reigns supreme but now quietly. The pilgrims, some of whom have up to a week's return journey on foot ahead of them, shuffle off to their final free hot breakfast. For all present the forty-five days of fasting are past; whether it be freshly slaughtered sheep or goat or modest chicken, the feasting beckons. And I too, grateful to be included, am invited to the feast.

Epiphany

Abyssinia Revisited: Letters from Lalibela

Scarcely recovered from its high-octane Christmas, Lalibela approaches Epiphany with renewed enthusiasm for public celebration. Even more streets are strung across with bunting in the Ethiopian colours of red, yellow and green, for, whereas Christmas is focussed in and around the churches, the Epiphany celebration is taken out to the people. And, happily, those people will now include Belinda, who flew in the day before yesterday to check up on me.

The afternoon prior to Epiphany marks the end of the market at which the feast is purchased for the morrow, and the start of ceremonies. After the ritual preparation for the removal of the tabots from the inner sanctuary in each of the eleven churches, strident horn calls from one church to another confirm that all churches are ready to combine forces around their treasured tabots; the moment has arrived for the appearance of the various processions. These issue forth from four different locations. From the main entrance to the larger group of churches, where a length of tired-looking red carpet is being rolled out, there emerges on either side a small army of national flag bearers, followed by a procession of children and young people clothed in gold and dark red and others in blue and white who constitute a combined choir complete with energetic leaders equipped with megaphones. Behind the carpet layers, behind the choir, behind the carpet sweepers, appears a host of outsize silk umbrellas:

Epiphany

white, scarlet, crimson, blue, green, multi-coloured, all embroidered with gold thread which glistens in the sunshine. Beneath the umbrellas parade with a dignity commensurate with their magnificent vestments priests in gold and silver robes, priests in scarlet and gold robes, deacons in black capes and white turbans, almost all bearing large, ornate crosses of wood or silver. Those who carry no cross are swinging censors. Deacons in white and red robes flank the procession, which moves forward at a stately pace dictated by the time it takes for the carpet layers to roll up the carpet from behind the procession, jog past the procession, deposit and unroll the carpet in front of the procession. It looks like the equivalent in perpetual motion of bringing up the rear of the Lord Mayor's Show, and rather more energetic.

The crowd falls in behind the procession, multiplying with their lesser umbrellas the impression, gained from a higher vantage point along the route, of a Roman tortoise's advance on a stronghold. But despite the pomp and the pageantry there is no suggestion of military precision; clergy join in with the chanting led by the choir in the vanguard; energetic drummers dance back and forth; spectators ululate, clap and sing in participation. It looks like a carnival procession. And yet along with the exuberance, the horns, the ululations, the communal singing and chanting, there is also a reverence mixed in with this joy. For almost concealed in the midst of the extravagance are those priests carrying on their heads the tabots, replicas of the tablets of stone which are the foundation of our religion, and which are believed by Ethiopians to be housed still in the original ark of the covenant in Axum, some 250 miles north of here. The tabots are wrapped in precious silk which hangs down behind the bearer's head, reaching almost to the ground; the honour of bearing the tabots is reflected in the serious demeanour of the senior priests given this task. Onlookers cross themselves as the tabots pass by; for a moment reverence trumps exaltation.

The procession reaches a junction where a smaller gathering of priests and deacons bearing the tabots from the more isolated St George's church waits in dignified splendour for the moment when it can swell the numbers. Passers-by bow and reverence the cross and tabots. In contrast, only a few yards away, unruly-looking young men dance around in a circle, waving, and occasionally clashing, sticks above their heads; it is the time of year to impress female onlookers. Their boisterous chanting of the joyful chorus "A Ya Ya" could so easily in a different setting be understood to threaten bellicose intentions; their appearance instantly reminiscent of those fuzzy-wuzzy natives who not so very long ago gallantly tried with their spears to defy the guns of General Napier at Magdala.

Two hundred yards further down the road the stately procession from St Michael's church can be seen descending over the uneven rock, worn smooth by countless feet over the centuries, to take its place in the ever-lengthening parade. Half an hour later the final conjunction of the main procession and the representatives from the second group of churches takes place in colourful confusion. By this time some tourists find themselves caught up in the procession, a few quite deliberately, their powerful camera lenses thrust into the very faces of the dignitaries. These foreign visitors make themselves conspicuous by their dress, their antics and their corpulence. One is ashamed, on this occasion and again in subsequent days, of their insensitivity to the religious nature of these events. The two processions, complete with their entourages, finally merge with happy disregard of pomp and circumstance, and the battalion of sparkling umbrellas, now preceded by several different groups of shouting dancers, and succeeded by hundreds of bell-ringing, horn-blowing, clapping camp followers, heads towards the ground set aside for the celebration of Epiphany.

Camels and wise men have no place in the Ethiopian Orthodox celebration of Epiphany; the focal point is the revelation of Jesus as God's Son at his baptism in the Jordan. Lalibela has its own River Jordan. In theory this is where the tabots should be taken, to be guarded overnight before the Mass begins at dawn. Unfortunately, at Epiphany time this Jordan is but a trickle through a steep and barely accessible gorge, completely unsuitable for a place of pilgrimage and tourism. One can imagine the soul-searching when the decision was taken to construct an artificial pool around which the service can be attended by hundreds (although no doubt some were consoled by the thought of the satisfyingly large amount of entrance money which tourists could be charged to witness proceedings). At least the pool is in the shape of a cross. Today the half-full pool earns scarcely a glance as both tabot and flag bearers process over the bare, greenery-strewn ground, to the accompaniment now of traditional religious chanting, to assemble in front of a large tent at the far end of the ground. A service of dedication begins; families talk; mobile phones ring; at the pool end of the ground young people dance still. The juxtaposition of excitement and reverence still surprises.

The keeping of the night vigil is not a silent affair. The droning of the prayers floats across the valley throughout the night. By dawn the Mass is underway: much chanting and swaying by walls of deacons, much praying by a phalanx of priests, much preaching by one enthusiastic orator. Finally a trio of venerables, consisting of the bishop and two priests, troop round to the four arms of the cross to bless each one by dipping their hand crosses in the water. They have to stoop low; it seems that the hose pipe responsible for filling the pool has been subject in the last few days to the same water supply restrictions as the long-suffering residents. The risk of breaking a bone does not deter the younger men of the congregation from enjoying the climax of the service; jumping in, some still fully clad, they enthusiastically take it upon themselves to splash the assembled onlookers with the sanctified water. Amid increasingly chaotic scenes the deacons seize the hosepipe and direct it onto their flock. Most are only too willing to welcome the cold shower, even at this chilly early morning hour; after all, this is the justification for the feasting to which they have been looking forward; a small price to pay for tucking into a leg of lamb.

The procession later this morning to return the tabots to their churches is the occasion of just as much jubilation as the preceding day. For a moment, however, the atmosphere threatens to sour. As the flag bearers, young people, priests and deacons turn out onto the road, a truck carrying more than a dozen paramilitary federal policemen arrives at some speed and stops twenty yards short of the procession. The occupants jump out, brandishing batons. They look as though they mean business as they advance toward the procession. Can they not tell the difference between a joyful celebration and an angry demonstration? The fears of a confrontation, even a beating, are not realised, however. These keepers of law and order, unlike the discreet, friendly local police, like to be seen to play a role in the front line. This time they are performing a protective role; from whom is not clear; the obtrusive foreigners should be likely candidates, but they seem to be untouchable. By this time the deacons in red and white have taken their place high above the road on a long wall; their counterparts in black capes are lined up in the road; chants to a swaying, dancing movement and to the accompaniment of the hand-held sistrum pass back and forth between the two groups. For a moment I am reminded of the alternation in the singing of psalms between the two sides of our choir at St Martin's; I make a mental note to investigate the purchase of sistra.

Lalibelans are dressed in their finery today, including us. Arrayed in traditional Ethiopian celebratory clothes, Belinda with her head veiled in white, we do our best to blend in inconspicuously with the throng. The colourful extravaganza continues for several more hours, making its way very slowly back up the hill, with stops here and there for displays of dancing, in their very different ways, by both deacons and by young men. And yet, when the tabots are finally restored to their homes, concealed behind silk curtains where only the priest may enter, the celebration is still not at an end. Tomorrow will be another occasion for a public holiday: St Mary's Epiphany day, an only slightly more modest affair, with solid support from the other churches; leading the procession, a huge picture of the Virgin; bringing up the rear, but asserting their presence with determination, dancing women of a certain age. And next week will be ever-popular St George's Epiphany celebration, climaxing around the cruciform church

Epiphany

with lovely, open views to the mountains. Yet another public holiday; yet another occasion for the young men to let off steam; yet more colour, more confirmation of the Lalibelan identity, more chaotic exuberance. The spectre of the looming fifty-four days of the Lenten fast is held, for a few more days, determinedly at bay.

A Wedding

The season between Epiphany and Lent is the wedding season. As many as ten weddings can take place on the same Sunday, even in a town as small as Lalibela. Since these invariably entail processions of decorated vehicles asserting the distinction of their occupants by the raucous blaring of horns, there is little chance at this time of the year of a quiet post-prandial Sunday afternoon nap; on the other hand, since almost every inhabitant will know at least one of the families involved, there is every chance that, as a guest at one or other of the weddings, he will himself be contributing to the hullabaloo. And should the extent of his social connections make a choice an uncomfortable necessity, he will derive consolation from the fact that he will be just as warmly received at the continuing celebrations of a second, or indeed a third, wedding the following day. For the families of the couple the reputation of the house is at stake: putting on a good show is paramount.

The invitation to one of these weddings was as unexpected as it was generous. Invited by my teacher friend, Atinkute, I had met neither the bride nor the groom, the latter being Atinkute's brother-in-law. Since Belinda would still be in Lalibela, she too was automatically included in the invitation. More surprisingly, the invitation was further extended to a friend of ours from Addis who, by chance, was due to be visiting us that weekend, although no-one would have an inkling as to who she was or why she was there.

A Wedding

In the late afternoon before the wedding we got a glimpse of what this liberality meant in practice. Beneath a temporary awning strung up above the yard, the compound which included my friend's house was filled with about thirty women; one or two were engaged with washing table linen in a large, shallow metal bowl of the type to be seen outside every home; the majority were seated at tables, their faces lighting up as they gave us a welcoming smile, while their hands wielded with easy expertise fearsome butchers' scimitars; various limbs of now unidentifiable animals were the subject of their industry, the resultant chunks of flesh tossed into large vats. Up on the dirt road overlooking the compound, vehicular access was today denied in favour of the erection, as yet far from complete, of a marquee of generous proportions, which reduced the width of the road by nine-tenths; benches and chairs were being assembled by a small army of male friends and neighbours to form rows facing a dais at the further end.

By the seventh hour of the following day the fruits of these laborious preparations were ready to be savoured. At first sight, the marquee, with its formal arrangement of chairs, now resembled a prep school prize-giving; the atmosphere was, however, anything but formal. Lively Ethiopian music filled the tent through loudspeakers; the dirt floor was strewn with greenery; the dais was gaily festooned with balloons and tinselly Christmas decorations of the type no longer fashionable at home. A number of more comfortable chairs were arranged at the back of the dais. Suspended behind the centrally placed small sofa was a giant photo of the couple to be married; since they were pictured already smiling ecstatically in their wedding outfits one could be forgiven for fearing one had missed the nuptials themselves. Not to be outdone, Belinda and I had arrived in clothing fit for the occasion: traditional Ethiopian dress, largely white, with colourful additions, and sandal-like white shoes; yet again our "sons" had looked after us. Despite or because of looking like a couple out of pantomime, we were shown to a seat at the front. There seems to be an unspoken convention that honoured guests should be placed immediately in front of the loudspeaker. A plate of food was soon delivered to us: injera, of course, with a hot beef wot and a cooler potato accompaniment; home-made barley beer was in constant supply; water was, thankfully, also offered. My prime concern both here and later became the preservation of my pristine white suit from contact with the pernicious orange colour of the wot.

The dais party had by now arrived: the groom was dressed in a white jacket and red bow tie; his supporters mostly sported black jackets with black bow ties. Those wearing a conventional black tie were dressed, on the one hand appropriately funereally, given the groom's lack of obvious gaiety; on the other strikingly at variance

A Wedding

with the exuberant dancing which soon broke out once the live music began. There is, it seems, no such thing as an Ethiopian crooner; it is upbeat or nothing; an insistent, Middle Eastern influenced, wailing call to an irregular, foot-stamping, shoulder-shaking beat accompanied by copious whoops and ululations. After a half hour of jollity, a solemn moment: bowing low in front of each senior family member in the front row, the dais party, headed by the groom, received in turn the traditional blessing before the marriage. The first part of the ceremony was complete.

I have made no mention so far of the bride; this is because the bride's family simultaneously hosts a similar reception for family and friends. It was to this second gathering that the groom, his supporters and guests now repaired; his family stayed behind to prepare a welcome for the bride, who would be presented to them by the groom later in the day. The procession of minibuses was assembled; a camera crew climbed on top of one to record the parade; the town centre was satisfactorily alerted to the happy occasion by hooting and loud music; Ephrem's minibus, in which we were being conveyed, rather less satisfactorily came off the road; a few onlookers lent a hand and a shoulder to hoist back onto the cobblestones the front wheel now suspended over the void to the side of the road; the consequent suspension of the rear wheel over an even steeper drop brought more onlookers to join the party; boulders were assembled and set beneath the errant wheel; thanks to their exertions, we eventually lurched off to rediscover the vanished procession. The tented compound at which we finally arrived occupied only half of the width of the road. It was enclosed by a forbidding corrugated iron fence; only the entrance at the far end announced by its display of paper chains and greenery that this was not a refugee camp. The groom's party advanced confidently and cheerfully on the entrance to the bride's house: they, buoyed with expectation; she, inside, waiting in feigned modesty to be claimed.

Once again seated in a position of honour, this time on the dais itself, we had a perfect view of the entrance of the couple. Two flowers girls in red daintily strewed imitation rose petals in their way. The bride, in white, her head uncovered but for a veil worn on the back of her head, looked happy, as well she might, being the centre of attention; her attendants in green looked concerned as the big-fat-gipsy-wedding-style dress threatened to envelop on its progress through the tightly packed rows some of the more fragile seated guests; the groom remained resolutely impassive. In contrast to the plastic flowers on the low table set before the conjugal sofa on the dais the bride's bouquet was composed of real flowers of red and orange. Laid over the table, the Israeli flag made a convenient, if rather puzzling, aesthetic contribution to the blue and white colour scheme of the

A Wedding

dais. Red, green, yellow, orange, blue; colour had been liberally dispersed, to the satisfaction of all.

The marriage was performed by a trio of monk, priest and deacon. It was a quietly uttered blessing. The monk joined the hands together and recited the prayers; rings were discovered by each of the betrothed in the two flower baskets; fingers were embellished in the conventional way; ululations greeted the union. Cloths were removed from a table near the dais, exposing an array of dishes of meat, vegetable and fruit; and, of course, injera, the Ethiopian equivalent of cutlery. Ethiopians may well be unique in their table manner of gradually consuming not only the food itself but simultaneously the means of feeding themselves. After the buffet, more dancing, more blaring horns, more joyful ululations. The groom at last managed a smile.

After another half hour this second assembly came to an end. It was time for the second family blessing, this time of the bride's party, headed by the couple newly joined in matrimony. Rice appeared to be thrown over the departing couple, but on closer inspection turned out to be polystyrene. The wide, hooped dress was pushed, cajoled and manoeuvred through the crowded marquee until successfully out on the road for more photographs. We did not linger to observe the next challenge of effecting the entry of the bride into a minibus. Our part in the celebrations was complete; to the remaining festivities back at the groom's house we were not invited. With a genuine gratitude for having been generously included in this major social occasion we took leave of out hosts. In the best tradition of Ethiopian weddings they had successfully upheld the families' honour by putting on a good show - reflected in the number of invitations issued, vehicles mustered and livestock slaughtered - and by concealing the prospect of months of subsequent austerity.

A Walk in the Country

Abyssinia Revisited: Letters from Lalibela

In the week following the excitement of Epiphany we booked to go on a peaceful guided walk in the highland countryside nearby. Going for a walk is, of course, not the same thing as walking to go somewhere. The latter is an unavoidable feature of life here, whether several miles to school and back every day, or many miles once a week to market, or as many as fifty and back on annual pilgrimage. Going for a walk, by contrast, can be a delight, a leisure activity free of any financial challenge, open to all. Here, at 3,000 metres, it has become known as trekking. The new name, doubtless adopted at some tourism promotion conference, aggrandises, popularises, romanticises. The activity itself remains a simple, age-old pleasure.

Belinda and I set off one day shortly after noon behind our two local guides and the donkey they had provided to carry our overnight bags. We had that morning enjoyed a spectacular drive through farming country, which, we realised only after the final ascent of a steep and seemingly never-ending hill, was definitely lowland country, even though at 6,000 feet it was nearly twice as high as Snowdon. Now elevated into the highlands, we were surprised and relieved to find that oxygen masks were not a prerequisite for normal activity; that in fact, once deprived of the view over the way we had come, there was little to mark the fact that we were now at around 10,000 feet. Villages functioned normally along the roadside; people walked their daily

A Walk in the Country

way without getting breathless; animals grazed the land with no sign of distress. So off we set. Our way took us along uneven paths shaded by lines of eucalyptus trees; past well-organised farming cottages with outhouses, some of which displayed a tin or plastic mug upside down on a stick, an invitation to enter and consume their barley beer; through cool copses of juniper surrounding a local church; over open grazing land where mixed herds of oxen, donkeys and goats were in charge of five-year-olds. At one point a large primary school to our left emitted a flood of children, who streamed towards the novelty of strangers passing through their land. These were simple, curious, friendly children, not like the more streetwise types of Lalibela.

Our walk continued like this over gently undulating country for three days. We became aware of why Abyssinia had probably never seen a wheeled vehicle before the construction of the Franco-Ethiopian Railway between Djibouti and Addis Ababa one hundred years ago; the tracks were either rocky, very rocky or of a sandy dust into which any wheel would sink, particularly in the wet season. The donkey or mule still reigns supreme here. Sometimes the path would be carpeted by eucalyptus leaves in shades of dark green and faded purple. It was tempting to draw a parallel with the mix of colours favoured by local women for their dress. Both sexes were employed on the land; the job of fetching water, as was that of making barley beer, was evidently reserved for women; that of threshing and winnowing for men. Impressive efforts at the newer science of terracing were shared between the sexes, perhaps a recognition in this traditional farming community that the modern world is more unisex than previous generations had thought possible. By contrast, the one village meeting we saw, which, we were told, had been convened to discuss the construction of a new church, was attended only by men. It was a return to pastoral, pre-industrial England or nineteenth century rural France. The impression was underscored by the pride with which we were shown one community's investment in a grinding machine; the figure astride the top of the frame, gradually pouring grain into the funnel, could have featured in a novel by Stendhal or George Eliot.

So was an inexpert curiosity about antiquated farming methods the only interest to sustain three days of walking? Not at all. The terrain had played a trick on us. That first evening, lulled into a feeling that here was a countryside in which we could feel comfortable, we walked towards the sinking sun, pausing to take a photograph of a herdsman and cattle silhouetted against the evening sky; little did we suspect that a few yards beyond our picturesque subject was a sudden perpendicular drop of thousands of feet. The change from undulating pasture to dramatic rift valley was as impressive as it was unexpected. It was as though we were suddenly granted a pilot's eye view, looking down

A Walk in the Country

from an aircraft temporarily suspended in mid-flight. Far below were small communities set amidst farming land that ranged over every hillside, plateau and valley that was conceivably farmable, and some that were not. At intervals across the landscape the conical roofs of round, apparently isolated churches could be descried, often atop a hemispherical hill. To the west, across the yawning void, the distant plateau which was the continuation of the high ground on which we stood was about to act as the sun's momentary resting place before dusk, so we were urged to follow the cliff edge path a short distance to our own refuge for the night, one of three tukuls built on a promontory which gave an even wider, 270 degree view over the remarkable rift valley landscape below. Tea and pancakes with honey was served on the very edge of the precipice. An inspection of the specially built lavatory tukul was made before nightfall. A location any nearer to the cliff edge would have been deemed unsafe, even here in Ethiopia. Mounting half a dozen steps, one turned and paused; the view through the stable door from this most exquisitely positioned throne was breathtaking, a seat surely superior to that of any regal throne, however palatial.

Dinner was served in the neighbouring tukul, in complete darkness other than by the light of a central fire: an excellent home-made vegetable soup, and a chicken wot – or so we were told; the shadows cast by the firelight forbade any close inspection. By this time we were as glad of the fire's warmth as of its flickering light. Outside, undimmed by even the minimal light pollution to be found in the relative metropolis of Lalibela, countless stars within and to either side of the Milky Way revealed themselves amid the sky's rich blackness. We retired early to bed, dressing ourselves in layers of clothes not normally associated with bedtime. Torches lay at the ready for the eventuality that a trip to the smaller tukul in the middle of the night might be required; in the event we survived the challenge and were rewarded with the sight of the late arrival of the moon hanging in the night sky, and at dawn a most memorably colourful sunrise. After a breakfast of tea, egg, bread and more local honey we reloaded our packs onto the donkey and took our leave of this most wonderful guest house; of the spectacular view; of our modest hosts from the local community; of the local baboons who danced over to see us safely away.

We feared that our walk had peaked too early; that nothing could compare with this unforgettable location. Our fears were unfounded. At lunchtime each day we arrived at a similarly dramatically positioned tukul where a hot meal awaited us. By the late afternoon of the second day we had traversed the breadth of what we now realised was a long, thin east-west plateau, to discover another stunning view over the farming communities of the lowland below, and another cliff-edge tukul

A Walk in the Country

guest house. The third night offered yet another similar treat. The days were filled with views of rural life, both human - friendly and skilled, particularly the boy who meticulously sewed up a gaping shoe leather for me - and natural – now wild and rocky, now domesticated with a variety of trees, flowers and butterflies it would have been a pleasure to chronicle. Our walk in the country, at first evoking a familiar pleasure, had proved to be rather more surprising and delightful than we had expected - but not because it bore the grandiose title of a trek.

You Are Old, Father Laurence

*What I Should Have Replied To Tadiso When He
(bluntly but so solicitously) Pointed Out That I Was OLD
- with apologies to Lewis Carroll -*

"You are old, father Laurence," young Tadiso said,
"And your hair has become very white,
And yet you so rarely cover your head –
Do you think, in this sun, it is right?"

"In my youth," father Laurence replied to his "son",
"I feared it might injure the brain;
But now that I'm perfectly sure I have none
I expose it to sun and to rain."

"You are old" said the youth, "as I mentioned before,
Yet you insist on striding around.
Do you think this is why you are panting much more –
I'm afraid you may drop to the ground."

"In my youth," said the sage, as he shook his white locks,
"Too much study broadened my chassis.
It's now my ambition to run like a fox,
Like your Heile Gebreselassie."

"You are old," said the youth, "and your wallet's so thin –
It scarcely contains any notes;
Yet you're back from the market with a happy, broad grin –
Pray, why did you buy twenty goats?"

"In my youth," said his teacher, "A miser was I,
Refusing to let money go.
But how d'you say "No" to these vendors so sly
In a language with no word for "No"!?

A Second Wedding

Two weddings in two weeks! This week I was consoled after Belinda's return home by an invitation to a wedding of a different nature from the first one. The prospective husband, Abiy's cousin, is a deacon. Deacons and priests are married in church at the very start of the day of conjugal festivities. I ascertained the hour at which the service would begin; despite my acquaintance with the early hour of the Orthodox Mass, I was a little taken aback to be told that I should be there by the start of the day, i.e. by 6 am international time. Accordingly, wrapped in ecclesiastical white prayer shawl, I set out in good time beneath the vast, starlit sky; very few people were about as I walked for twenty minutes towards the churches. I confess I wondered whether this wasn't some prank being played on me.

At the entrance to the church of St Mary the thought reasserted itself; nobody was there to meet me, as I thought had been agreed. I listened to muffled chanting from within as I waited anxiously. The hour was approaching, so I decided I had better venture up the deep passageway cut through the rock, which led to an ancient door at the top of some well-worn steps. I followed an elderly woman who slipped off her shoes at a second doorway. I did likewise, although I soon saw that we had gained access only to the sunken surround of the church. To the left and right were worshippers, not hugely numerous, only some of whom, I noticed in my concern to conform to convention, had removed their

A Second Wedding

shoes. I found myself opposite the women's entrance to the church, easily discernible from the huddle of veiled female forms under the porch. I should have to walk over the uneven rocky floor around to the far side of the church. I felt more than a little conspicuous. To my left, in the wider carpeted space opposite the priests' entrance, picturesquely arrayed behind a set of traditional drums set out on the floor, deacons assumed a variety of postures: some were erect, reading their Bible or prayer book; rather more were semi-recumbent, propped up against the rock wall; a few looked as though they had altogether succumbed to fatigue. To make my way across this designated space was a forbidding prospect.

Unsure how to proceed, I was relieved to see two more Westerners, appropriately dressed, appear with an Ethiopian guide. On enquiry I found that he was one of the many deacons who act as guides, and yes, he knew that his colleague, Alebachew, was getting married today to Abeba (which in translation is "Flower" – female names are altogether more attractive than their male counterparts; men's names I came across included "I See", "The Door", "Don't Touch Him" and "Another One".) However, the Mass, he informed me, had started at 5.30 am; nobody could enter after the start of the service. I felt a little let down. From my new vantage point I found I could see through the women's entrance a little more of the interior; a cloud of incense enveloped two heads crowned in white and gold. Thereafter, as the numbers of worshippers greatly increased with the break of day, I doggedly defended my position in this women's area until the number of women clogging the entrance forbade any view at all. In the intervening period the number of crowned heads inside had increased to four. I recalled talk of two couples being married simultaneously. The bell hanging in an arched recess before the main entrance was rung; worshippers dropped to their knees; at some communally understood moment all struggled to their feet again, only for the practice to be repeated twice more. A black bird with orange underparts aggressively asserted its territorial rights to the porch above the women; a baby's crying could only be assuaged by the young mother pushing her way forward to find blessed relief on the very threshold of the church; the occasional banal ring tone from a mobile phone provided a third distraction from the chanting within. After two hours I decided little more was to be gained from further attendance. Forsaking any chance of joining the newly-weds for the wedding breakfast, quite possibly still another hour or two away, I retired from the throng and walked home, disconsolate. I later learned that Alebachew and Abeba had been married at 3 am.

Early in the afternoon, kitted out once again in my Ethiopian wedding attire and correctly informed of the hour, I duly arrived at the first reception at the groom's

A Second Wedding

family house. The bride was nowhere to be seen, having, despite her so recently attained marital status, been reclaimed by her family. The large tented area was this time not in the road but on ground adjacent to the groom's father's house. The sloping ground proved a challenge to the arrangement of the chairs; despite this a delicious beef stew and talla, the local home-made beer, were served without mishap. Before us the equivalent of the dais was attractively and colourfully decorated; around and above us the many bare wooden supports of the canopy were decorously wrapped in toilet paper and further adorned with greenery. The groom's supporters seemed to be all deacons, conspicuous in their white and red robes and white turbans. They were a jolly lot. Their inclination to dance was all too obvious, even to the popular secular Ethiopian music with which we were at this early juncture serenaded.

The procession of eight minibuses, preceded by four tuk-tuks, was grander than any rival parade we encountered on our hour-long tour of the town; the generous hooting turned the heads of all and sundry; the spontaneous singing from within the buses attracted smiles on every side. This was indeed a relatively musical cacophony. The procession finally arrived at the bride's family house; horns were blown; the groom's clerical supporters went into overdrive, singing, clapping and dancing their way up to the tented area. They took their places either side of the sofa on which sat the groom, clutching his bouquet of yellow, blue and white flowers, alongside his best man, who at this time was dressed in white and gold in an apparent usurpation of the bride's role. When everyone was settled, it was time for the next excitement: the collection of the bride, or more correctly, the wife. The groom, best man and deacons set off for the house. This time I was encouraged to join the party. Propelled into a small, thronged, typically windowless room, I was somewhat disappointed not to see a rapacious claiming of a reluctant bride. The couple, both resplendent in white and gold crowns and capes, the bride's hair modestly concealed beneath her veil, were sitting pacifically next to one another, smiling somewhat self-consciously for the cameras. A large leg of mutton was flourished in front of them. A piece was carved and handed to the groom, who fed it manually to his lady with all the authority of one several years older than his bride, a commonplace here. The process was repeated in reverse. The validity of the marriage apparently thus confirmed, the bride received her flowers from the groom, who did not present his bouquet in toto to the bride but shared it equally with her. The couple were then escorted amidst ululations and horn-blowing to the marquee, where, after a jolly circular dance by the deacons, celebrating, like their matrimonial rings, the infinity of the commitment, they took their places on the connubial sofa.

A Second Wedding

The second course of the wedding feast was served. At one point another joint of meat was produced with a flourish for the delectation of the dais party, of which I was again, to my embarrassment, one: this prime cut of goat was once again fed first by the groom to his bride and then in reverse. The ritual offering of meats in a tabernacle amid so many priests and deacons all seemed a bit Old Testament. There followed the equivalent of after-dinner speeches and entertainment: a deacon declaimed a well-received celebratory poem in the couple's honour; the groom stood to be prayed over, the monotone chant occasionally subverted by spontaneous, and apparently humorous, interventions of a non-prayerful character; the deacons, to the accompaniment of a singer and the masinko, performed several energetic dances, one of which resembled an amusing courtship dance. I wondered if ministry training for the Church of England should not incorporate this in order to liven up the wedding package.

Eventually it was time to leave the bridal home. The couple were escorted noisily into the road; guests, more numerous now, even though the bride's family remained at their home, squeezed into the waiting festooned vehicles; the film crew mounted one of the minibuses; the huge, woven injera container, traditional symbol of the new household, was hoisted onto the roof of the marital minibus; the procession set off, alerting the neighbourhood in the traditional, rowdy way to the transfer of the bride to her new family.

Drawing near to the groom's family home, the procession turned into the forecourt of a tourist hotel. Pale faces appeared on balconies to investigate the reason for the commotion. The couple posed in their wedding finery for formal photographs; hotel guests' cameras were busy as their owners swelled the procession on foot through the grounds to a table which was decorated and set for the newly-weds, dominated by a three-tier iced wedding cake and a bottle of wine. A little bit of England amid the poinsettia bushes and jacaranda trees. The fizzing and explosion of hand-held Roman candles accompanied the lighting of those on the cake itself, adding to the gaiety of the moment. After the ritual cutting of the cake and the third feeding of one another, the couple sat down to be served, while drink and cake were dispensed to all onlookers, including the delighted hotel guests. Then, as dusk fell, the congregation continued on foot to the house of the groom, the couple silhouetted against the darkening sky under a ceremonial Timkat umbrella. The long day was drawing to a close, but the celebrations would continue for some hours yet this evening, and beyond; guests would be welcome to call during the subsequent days until the two families would finally be united at the last feast seven days later.

A Second Wedding

As I took my place once more under the attractively decorated canopy for an evening buffet of meat, salad and fruit, by now accompanied by Abiy, Yosef and Ephrem, I realised that, after the immense communal effort to prepare this celebration, almost everybody I had ever met in this area of the town was here, from my night-watchman to the proprietor of the Jerusalem Hotel, from the owner of my rented house to my young tuk-tuk driver friend, either engaged in serving the refreshments or simply enjoying the festive ambience. This inclusiveness was a definitive display of the community values which underpin and enrich life here; amid the insecurity and anxiety which attend daily life for so many, an essential rock on which this society is built and continues to function.

Goodbye to Lalibela

Abyssinia Revisited: Letters from Lalibela

One final letter, mercifully short: after twelve weeks it's time to say goodbye to Lalibela.

It's goodbye most poignantly of course, to our three "sons", who have at all times been wonderfully solicitous, diligent and caring. And then it's goodbye too to the daily sunshine and the overawing night sky; it's goodbye to steep-sided gorges and flat-topped mountains; it's goodbye to palms, eucalyptus and cactus; it's goodbye to cocks crowing, hens clucking, donkeys braying; its goodbye to the deferential bow of the head to and from the stranger in the street; it's goodbye to poinsettia, bougainvillea and jacaranda; it's goodbye to donkeys, mules and tuk-tuks; it's goodbye to injera, shiro and wot. It's goodbye to the combination of poverty, pride and piety; it's goodbye to the spontaneous and joyful celebration of life's better moments; it's goodbye to dancing deacons; it's goodbye to the shoulder-dance, the masinko, the ululation; it's goodbye to appreciative pupils; it's goodbye to supportive colleagues, friends and neighbours; it's goodbye to automatic respect; it's goodbye to the land of easy smiles.

But it's also goodbye to the frying pan which will balance on the electric ring only when supported by a packet of tea bags wedged under the handle; it's goodbye to the bedroom curtain which falls down at the slightest touch; it's goodbye to taps which promise the delivery of water but continually disappoint; it's goodbye to the washing line which is accessible only by clambering

Goodbye to Lalibela

over a barrier of breeze blocks; it's goodbye to picks and shovels and dust. It's goodbye to the meaningless Ethiopian driving licence; it's goodbye to the occasional power cut and to frustrating, intermittent wi-fi; it's goodbye to pesky flies, bedbugs and scorpions; it's goodbye to charming but brazen children interested only in a handout; it's goodbye to two-level pricing; it's goodbye to scruffy, littered classrooms such as would cause a traditional schoolmaster an instant attack of apoplexy; it's goodbye to the potentially boundless throng of people finding life difficult.

And it's farewell to the most exhilarating and enriching three-month period of my last twenty-five years.

www.ingramcontent.com/pod-product-compliance
Lightning Source LLC
Chambersburg PA
CBHW031114080526
44587CB00011B/965